C000263861

Obex Publishing Limited
Reg. No. **12169917**

CONTENTS

I am totally passionate about baking and creating easy, fuss free, simple bakes that not only taste brilliant but look like a show stopper too! I believe everyone can bake something yummy and decorate it to look fantastic. You won't need a load of fancy tins or expensive tools of the trade. Just a very basic set of equipment is all you need to get started.

In this book, I hope to bring you the best of the baking and decorating worlds. Delicious tasty treats perfect for all kind of celebrations and family get togethers, combined with some easy to follow decorating tutorials. You'll find simple tray bakes for a quick morning baking before seeing friends for lunch, or more decorated cakes for parties and celebrations. This book will hopefully inspire you to get your bake on and wow your family and friends with your creations!

ABOUT ME

Hello! I'm Dani, I own, teach and am cake obsessed at Blue Door Bakery. I've run my own cake business since 2011 and I'm absolutely passionate about sharing my love of cake decorating and knowledge with you.

I'm 37. I've been married to Dean for 21 years and we have beautiful daughters, Mae and Lana who are 17 and 13. I live in Redditch, Worcestershire with 2 crazy dogs and an even crazier cat.

I began my love of cake decorating in 2011. Or you could say even before that. My Nan was an amazing cake decorator. I remember the days at her house when I was a pre teen making sugar flower displays, carnations and cakes. I remember the boozey smell of cakes that would fill her kitchen over the winter. Opening the cupboard door under her oven and deep, alcohol filled fruit cakes piled high wrapped in baking paper, and tin foil. She created hundreds of amazing cakes over the years for family and friends. My whole family is incredibly creative. My Nan made cakes, my Grandad loved painting, playing piano and guitar, my Uncle is an incredible artist and my amazing Mum is a children's book author. I seem to have passed the creative genes down to my 2 daughters too who love to draw, bake, paint and create.

When my daughters were younger, I needed something to do from home to fit around them and school runs. I came across Blue Door Bakery online. The company baked for orders and had just started teaching cake classes. I attended 2 classes with my Mum and you could safely say I was hooked! I had another 2 classes booked in for the summer of 2012 then received an email from BDB to ask if I had ever considered teaching cake classes and would I be interested in teaching for them. I'll never forget the excitement of receiving that email.

After meeting the BDB team, we arranged a few months of cake and class teaching tuition and I began teaching just 8 months after making my first cake. How crazy is that! But I found it came very naturally to me. Not only the skills needed but the patience to help those who attended my classes.

During the first few years of teaching, I was building up my cake business from home. I had started volunteering in a local first school and taking a teaching assistant course. So you could say I've always enjoyed teaching. Adults are a little easier to teach than children, I don't have to use the naughty step quite as much!

I soon left that job to focus full time on making and teaching cakes.

My first class was a little terrifying. Teaching 9 people how to bake and decorate cupcakes was totally out of my comfort zone. But it's crazy how we adapt and soon enough it became second nature to me. For almost 3 years I was teaching every week, creating new classes and building up my own business. I eventually became so busy with my business that I gave up doing celebration cakes and cupcakes and focused solely on wedding cakes and classes.

2 years later, BDB was up for sale and due to be purchased and franchised to York. A week before the sale was due to be finalised, it fell through. Honestly, it never even entered my mind to take over the business. I never thought I could. After a huge push and a lot of nagging from my husband I agreed to take over and buy the company. I'll forever be thankful to him for believing in me when I didn't believe in myself.

I took over total control and management of the company, moved premises and redesigned some classes. Then a short while after I purchased the company. I rebranded and made it my own.

My first studio in 2014 was a rented space in a pottery cafe. I knew this

was very temporary for me to get the business going. I was there for 6 months. It was great for me to teach classes and run the business my way however the space was so impractical. It was tiny. There was no storage space so everything was kept at my home and bought to each class in boxes. There was no parking so it meant parking at a local train station and a ton of journeys to load all the equipment in to the studio space. And the constant panic about what if I forgot something half way through a class was bad! It was definitely not a permanent place.

In 2015 a gorgeous local courtyard full of businesses had a room for rent. I went to have a look, it was super tiny but it was my own! It meant no sharing space with anyone and with careful planning, I had space to just about store everything I needed. It took a lot of work to get it looking smart and a big investment to fit a kitchen, ovens, plumbing, large work table etc. My husband is a very handy man to be married to as he did everything to make this room what it is. I loved my first little studio. It was where I really found my feet running a business. I redesigned all new classes in this studio, introduced a new range of online recipe tutorials and taught around 900 students in the 2 years I was there.

In 2017 the studio space next door came available. It was 4 times the size and had a separate storeroom. But it was run down, falling apart and generally not fit for food purpose at all. Again, my husband and his handy skills came to my rescue and after 2 weeks of plastering, fitting ceilings, flooring, kitchens, another oven, another fridge and a ton of pretty accessories and a major ikea trip

later.... It was totally fit for purpose and an absolute dream space.

I had this studio for just over 3 years. There was so much room for storing for my display cakes, equipment, tools and my growing collection of sprinkles. My students had so much space to work and learn during classes.

While I was in this studio, my business went crazy. I had over 1000 students per year from all over the world, Japan, New York and Greece as well as many people travelling from all over the UK to attend.

During the lockdown of 2020/2021 my business moved to all online. I spent months baking, teaching over zoom and on Facebook lives. Its been so popular that this side of my business is now bigger than ever! I now have a perfect home studio and teach everything online. I run online cake business courses ranging from a few days to a more personal course over a month which helps people begin their cake journey. I have online recipes, decorating guides, courses on cake social media, Instagram, food photography, cake pricing, sugar flowers, cake covering... the list goes on. As well as all this, I have built up my YouTube channel and IGTV account with so many free tutorials and information.

I write regular blog posts, sharing cake business help to emergency cake repair kits and everything in between. I have worked with Kenwood and Mary Berry on the promotion of their new range of stand mixers. I even got invited to London to their promotional event to meet the Queen of baking herself. I have been featured and interviewed in a regional magazine. I have been a regular contributor to Cake Decorating Heaven magazine, Baking Heaven magazine and also Cake Masters magazine, with many of my cakes appearing on the front cover. I've hosted Facebook live tutorials on social media accounts. And now, writing this book. Crazy!!

Honestly, my business wouldn't be what it is today if it wasn't for my students. They are an absolute joy. Not just teaching them but watching them expand their business, become busy with orders and grow their cake confidence. I've made more friends in this job than I ever thought I would. Its the best when my students become friends. I am forever grateful to them for their constant support, kindness and generally just being awesome people!

I hope you enjoy the recipes and the decorating tutorials. Now get your bake on! Feel free to get in touch with me on Instagram with any questions. You can find me @bluedoorbakery

Dani x

I'm going to give you the low down on baking ingredients, what they are, how best to use them and top tips throughout…

Before you start baking, make sure you have all the ingredients listed in the recipe. Honestly, I've lost count the number of times I've baked a cake and not had enough butter in stock or my baking powder is out of date. Double check your ingredients before you start. Also, it really helps to prepare your items too. Soften the butter, get the eggs and milk out the fridge to get to room temperature, make sure you have tea bags in and make yourself a cuppa! Then let's begin.

FLOUR

Some recipes use plain flour, some use self raising, some use plain flour and baking powder. Most of the time my preference is self raising flour for cakes. It's a standard measurement which you can't really go wrong with. If you need it a little more precise, recipe depending, you can use plain flour and baking powder. However, just stick to the recipe. A mid range flour brand from supermarkets works great and this is what I always use.

BAKING POWDER

Pay close attention to the use by date on this. If it has gone past or at least getting close to the date, you may find the rise of the cake isn't as good. Always use this as fresh as possible. Supermarkets sell this in small packets now which I feel is much better for hobby/small baking as it keeps it fresher.

SUGAR

Caster sugar is a refined white sugar that is commonly used for baking. It is important to use this instead of granulated sugar as it's much finer so the crystals of sugar melt better in the bake.

The brown sugar keeps hold of some moisture, so using it will result in baked goods that are softer yet denser. This makes it perfect to use in cookies for example.

Golden caster sugar gives your bake a slightly light brown colour and a more caramel flavour. It works a little like the dark brown sugars in keeping in a little of the moisture in the cake.

MILK

If using milk in a recipe, make sure it's whole milk and at room temperature. I keep UHT milk in stock as this way it's always at room temperature in my cupboard when needed.

EGGS

EGGS

All eggs used in the recipes are medium size, free range and at room temperature. An average medium size egg weighs approximately 55g so you can weigh it if you prefer but in my opinion there is no need.

BUTTER

For cakes you can either use baking spread/margarine or butter. If a recipe states using butter, please do so and I promise it'll make a yummy difference. Make sure it's at room temperature unless the recipe tells you different.

FLAVOURING

I will always recommend using extract instead of essence. It's a much stronger flavour. I prefer to invest in good flavourings rather than anything else. This is what will make a big difference to the yumminess of your cake.

COCOA POWDER

Always use the best cocoa powder you can. A brilliant supermarket brand is Green and Blacks but there are some great brands out there who produce really high quality and intense flavours.

CHOCOLATE

I always use Callebaut chocolate. This brand is fantastic quality when using it in cakes, buttercream or ganache. Its high cocoa solid content means it will work really well when adding it to your bakes. The better quality chocolate you can buy, the better it'll work for you in the recipe. Callebaut also sell cocoa powder which is fantastic too.

TEA

When baking it's very important to stay hydrated. I always have Yorkshire Tea bags. And I'd highly recommend these with a chocolate hobnob!

Over the years I have bought so much equipment and every time thought, Yep, I'll use this and never actually used it. So here are my go to cake bits and bobs that every baker needs that won't be a wasted purchase.

CAKE TINS

I always bake in at least 2 tins. If you have more, use them all! This way you'll have a much nicer, lighter and softer bake to your cake. Most of my cakes have 4 layers and I use 2 tins (approximately 3 inch deep). Just halve each cake once cooked and cooled then you are ready to layer up. All recipe timings in this book are for 2 tins. Bare in mind, if you are baking in lots of tins rather than a couple, your cooking time will be reduced. If baking in 3 or 4 tins, I'd recommend reducing the cooking time by 10 minutes. Just ensure you check it's cooked before removing from the oven.

When baking the recipes in this book, you should achieve approx 5 inch cake when stacked on a board or drum, layered with fillings and buttercream. No point having a small cake is there!

CUPCAKE TRAYS

I bake cupcakes in muffin trays using muffin cases. They are deeper than standard cupcake trays producing a bigger cupcake.

FOOD COLOURING

For colouring buttercream, the food colours you use must be concentrated. Liquid colours from the supermarket are just not concentrated enough to get a good colour. Plus, you also need to use so much that they change the consistency and taste of the buttercream. It's not good.

I really like the brand Colour Mill. These are such a fantastic range of colours and always on trend with the shades you can achieve. The majority of the cakes and bakes in this book use this brand of colour as I think they work brilliant with buttercream. I do also use Sugarflair gel colours for a slightly more depth to the colour. Sweet Sticks are fantastic for painting on buttercream too. Both can be purchased from online cake decorating shops. My go to website is cake-stuff.com

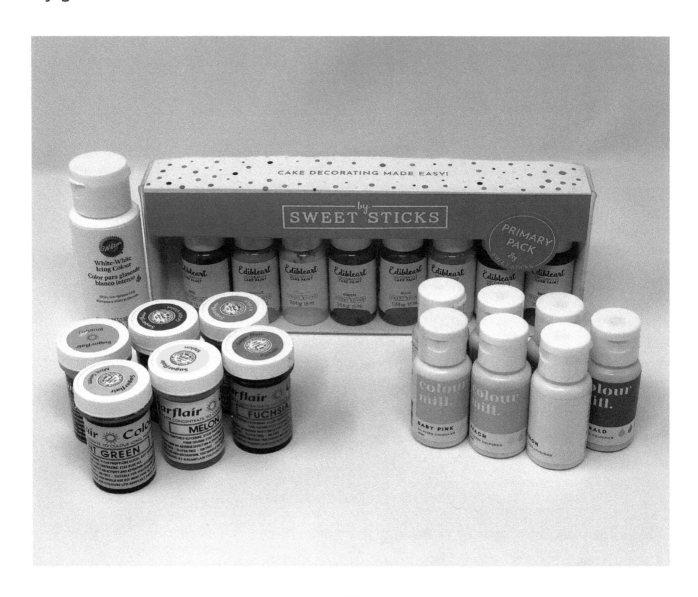

MEASURING SPOONS

A basic set of these is definitely a necessity. They are a precise measurement. If adding a measured spoon of ingredients, make sure it's flat or scrape off the excess with a knife.

ICE CREAM SCOOPS

These are amazing for ensuring each cupcake is the same size. It makes it so easy to pop the batter in each cupcake case without causing a total mess of your muffin tray. The scoop size I use is 56mm.

I also use these scoops a little later on in the book with my Triple Chocolate Cookie recipe. They are great for filling with cookie dough to get even size cookies every time.

PALETTE KNIFE

Standard size of around 4 inch is fine for all decorating techniques. It's great for spreading buttercream in layers or smoothing around a cake.

RUBBER SPATULA

You'll get at least 1 more cupcake of batter out of your mixing bowl if you use one of these to scrape out the excess. Unless you like to lick the bowl then don't bother!

CAKE LEVELLER

These are so good for getting even layers of cake. Using a large serrated knife is good but sometimes the cake ends up looking like a door stop rather than a level layer of cake. For just a few £££ these are an essential tool of mine.

SPRINKLES

I am completely sprinkle obsessed. They are my total guilty pleasure and I feel zero guilt when I've had a sprinkle splurge. If you need sprinkle advice, I'm your girl! I can recommend so many amazing sprinkle companies

Super Streusel - These are epic! The colours, range, shape... everything! Most of my bakes in this book have these sprinkles on. I love them.

Other great sprinkle companies -
Sprinkly UK
Sweet stamp
Sprinkletti

CUTTERS

You can purchase a huge variety of cake cutters now. This basic 5 petal flower is a great beginner. You can make all kinds of frilled flowers and roses with this one.

A LARGE METAL SCRAPER

I really like the scrapers from Finch Bakery. They are super tall and sturdy. They sell striped scrapers (see the chocolate stripe cake) but I also use the other straight side for all my smooth cakes. With metal scrapers, you can heat them up in some hot water to give your final coat of buttercream an extra smooth finish.

PIPING BAGS

I use disposable piping bags. I just don't think you can fully clean a reusable one properly.

PIPING NOZZLES

Any nozzle of your choosing can be used on any of the cakes. My preference is a Jem 2D. I find this is the best nozzle to use on any kind of buttercream swirls. I also love Wilton 104 for ruffles and any large open star nozzle for a different effect on swirls.

MIXER

If you have a stand mixer, always use this for your baking. They will make the cake batter in half the time and do all the hard work for you. I would always recommend using a paddle attachment for mixing the batter.

If you don't have a stand mixer, a hand held electric whisk is brilliant. Most large supermarkets will sell these for you to grab along side your ingredients and they are very affordable.

If you want to use me as an excuse to buy a stand mixer, then go right ahead!!

OTHER HANDY BITS AND BOBS

Edible Glue

Paintbrushes - size 2 and 4.

Cocktail sticks - for adding food colour into buttercream.

A selection of mixing bowls

Scissors

Spoons for mixing buttercream colours

SCALES

Digital scales make life so much easier. I'd recommend getting scales which weigh grams as well as mls.

CAKE DRUMS AND BOXES

You can buy these anywhere now, online, cake decorating shops and supermarkets. I love to use the white cake drums. I'm not a huge fan of the silver drums showing.

CUPCAKE CASES

I use Muffin cases, these are larger and deeper than regular cupcake cases. More cake is better right! Size 50-53mm base and 30-38mm deep.

TURNTABLE

You'll also really benefit from using a turntable. I use PME as it's very stable and you can tilt it making some decorating work easier.

I've learnt so much over the years with a ton of baking disasters to date. I've forgotten to add eggs, used twice as much baking powder as necessary, used salt instead of sugar (don't ask!!), opened the oven door too early and the cake has completely sunk... the list is endless.

So hopefully I can help you avoid as many cake fails as I had.

OVEN

Always switch your oven on before starting to prepare any ingredients. This way it has enough time to reach temperature before your goodies go in. All the recipes in this book are based on a fan oven.

PREPARATION

Get your ingredients out the cupboard and fridge, get your apron on and get your tins lined. Weigh out your ingredients and make sure items are at room temperature or microwave softened. Make a cup of tea then you can begin.

LINING YOUR TINS

Although lining your tins with baking paper is a bit of a pain, it's worth it. It saves tons of time washing the tins and makes it loads easier to get your cake out of the tin once cooked. The amount of times I haven't lined the tin properly and a section of the cake has stuck to the bottom of the tin causing me to re bake. I use vegetable oil spray to cover the inside of the tin. The stuff you use for your stir fry is perfect. Then line them with baking paper on the bottom and around the sides. It's worth it I promise.

Don't over mix your batter. It can cause the cake to become heavy and dense. Only mix until all the ingredients are just combined then you are good to go.

BAKING THE CAKE

Always bake in the centre of your oven. Every oven is very different so base cooking times suitable for your oven. In recipe timings in this book is a guideline however timings can vary up to 10-15 minutes either side. Please use your judgement on this and ensure you fully check the cake is cooked before taking out of the oven.

To check when your sponge cake is cooked, take it out of the oven and have a look at it. It should be a light, golden colour and the edges of the cake should be pulling away from the sides of the tin slightly. If you gently press

the middle it should feel slightly bouncy to the touch (not soggy). If you push a skewer into the middle of the cake it should come out clean and with no uncooked batter on it. If it's not cooked, pop it back in for another 5 minutes and then check again.

In my opinion big cakes tend to bake better at a lower oven temperature for a little longer. This is so that the outside isn't over cooked and the middle is not dry.

As a rule, if you feel that your big cakes are overdone and slightly hard on the outside, next time reduce your oven temperature by 10C and increase the cooking time by 10 minutes.

The recipe timings in this book are based on cooking in 2 tins. You could also bake in more tins which will give the cakes less time in the oven if you prefer. If baking in more tins than suggested, reduce the cooking time by 10 minutes then check if it is cooked.

Try not to open the oven door until the cake has been in for about 3/4 of the baking time you're expecting it to take. Opening the oven door too soon often ends in a sunken cake or uncooked doughy bakes.

I'd definitely recommend getting an oven thermometer so you can find out the true temperature of your oven. After a while your oven can lose a little of its power which may result in a lower temperature without you knowing it. Pop in a thermometer and this will make a big difference to the end result of your bakes knowing the temperature is true.

*Please remember that ovens vary a great deal, so you will need to adjust the temperature and/or cooking time for your own oven.

I use muffin tins and muffin cases. These are deeper than standard cupcake trays. Use a 56mm ice cream scoop to pop your batter in the cases so that each cupcake is as even as possible when baked.

Cupcakes do not take too long to cook. Once cooked, your cupcake should look golden brown (for vanilla flavour) on top and slight springy to touch. They should also feel dry. If they feel slightly wet, pop them back in for another 2 minutes. Keep them in the cupcake tray to cool for 5 minutes before removing.

STORING CAKES

Keep finished cakes in a cake box. Id recommend not storing in the fridge unless it's a buttercream finish cake and it's boiling hot. Otherwise somewhere cool is suitable. Obviously use your judgement on this, if buttercream is melting, it needs the fridge.

If you store the cake in tupperware it can cause the cakes to sweat due to lack of air flow. This can leave a wet finish to your fondant or pealing cupcake cases. A cake box is just fine.

You can also slice up big cakes, wrap these in cling film and store in the freezer for 6 weeks. This way, you can just take out a slice of cake when your sweet tooth is taking over.

EAT UP

For cupcakes I'd recommend eating within 2 days of baking. For big cakes I'd recommend within 5-7 days. Or just slice up and spread the cake love to family, friends and neighbours.

MASTERING THE BASICS

ALL ABOUT BUTTERCREAM

Buttercream is a sweet filling used on cakes or piled high on cupcakes. Traditionally this is made is 1 part butter and 2 parts icing sugar. Easy peasy right!! There are a few tricks of the trade to make it easier than ever.

BUTTER

I always use unsalted butter in buttercream. Butter is the only way to get the right taste, consistency, colour and texture. Also with using proper butter, not margarine for e.g., the buttercream sets better. It forms a slight crust and doesn't melt in warm weather as easy.

I don't believe the brand of butter you use makes a huge difference. I use which ever is on offer or cheapest at the time.

The best way to use the butter for buttercream is to soften it slightly in the microwave first (if you forget take it out the fridge in time to soften). It needs to be soft and squidgy, just like you left it at room temperature on warm day. Just basically try not to melt it!

FLAVOURINGS

Always add in the best flavourings you can. I use vanilla extract. It's my favourite and I find goes with most cake flavours.

If adding cocoa powder to buttercream to make it chocolate flavour, use the same cocoa powder as in your cakes. Just a tablespoon at a time until you are at the desired flavour and colour. There is no right or wrong amount to add. It's just personal preference. As you are adding in more cocoa powder, this may make the buttercream slightly stiffer. Make sure you add a little more boiling water to get it to the right consistency if needed.

The best way to achieve really white buttercream is to beat the butter on its own for as long as you can. You'll see it getting paler and paler. After you've added the icing sugar and if the buttercream is still slightly yellow, you can add in some food whitener. I use Wilton White White Icing Colour. Just squeeze in a bit at a time and mix. You'll soon see the colour start to lighten. As an alternative, you could add a tiny bit of purple food colouring which will reduce the yellow tones. Add a very small amount at a time though as it can very easily go from a yellow tone to a grey/lilac.

To get the best consistency for piping and smoothing, you'll need to add a few drops of boiling water. This makes it really light and fluffy. Use your judgement on this. Start off with a teaspoon of boiling water and see how you go.

If you have any left overs, it is easy to keep and reuse. Put any remaining buttercream in a bowl or tub. I'd recommend pressing some cling film down on to the surface of the buttercream before storing. It stops a crust forming as much.

Keep in the fridge for a few weeks or in the freezer for up to 6 weeks. Keep a note of the use by date for the butter too.

This will be enough to fill, stack, crumb coat and add a final layer on to a 6 inch round cake by 5 inches deep. Use approximately half this amount to decorate 12 cupcakes.

INGREDIENTS

400g unsalted butter

800g Icing sugar

1-3 teaspoons of boiling water (if needed)

Flavouring
(2 tsp of vanilla extract)

1. Begin by softening your butter in a microwave. Around 30 seconds per 250g block of butter (straight from the fridge) works for me however this may differ depending on the firmness of your butter and your microwave. Once soft, pop in your mixer and mix on the highest speed for 3-4 minutes.

2. Stop and scrape down your mixer bowl and you'll see how pale it has gone in colour.

   Mix up again for a few minutes. Weigh

out the icing sugar and add this in to the butter.

3. The best way to ensure you aren't breathing in a ton of icing sugar is to wrap your mixer with cling film. My mixer does come with a guard however I still prefer to cling film wrap as it stops any icing sugar coming out.

   This really helps to keep all the icing sugar clouds away.

   Once wrapped, mix this on high for 2-3 minutes.

4. Next, add in your flavouring and a little boiling water. If you are unsure of how much to add, (or not confident is pouring it in!) use a teaspoon and add this bit by bit until it's at the consistency you are happy with.

   Mix up on high.

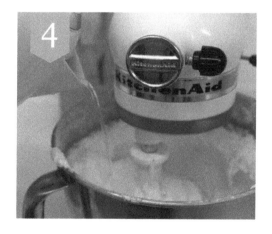

5. Lastly, I like to use Wilton White White Icing colour to take away some of the yellow tones and brighten the buttercream.

   Add in a squeeze and mix this on a high speed for a minute and you'll see this getting paler. Add in a little more if needed. You'll never get buttercream to be brilliant white but you'll get it off white instead of yellow.

   Ta-da! Read to pipe.

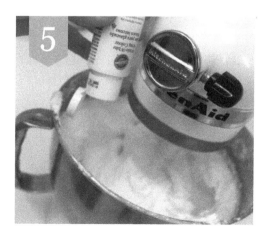

This is such a basic step but if you learn how to do it easily and it'll save you a lot of faff.

I use disposable piping bags and a wide range of nozzles. You'll also need a big jug/pot and some scissors.

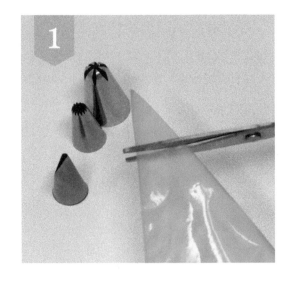

Start by snipping a little off the end of your piping bag. Just enough for the nozzle to poke out the end.

Insert your nozzle.

Then pop this piping bag inside your big jug or tub and fold the piping bag over the rim of this.

This will keep the bag open and give you both hands free to deal with your buttercream.

Take a spatula or big spoon and put some buttercream inside the piping bag.

Try not to put too much in. You want just enough that it feels comfortable to hold in your hand.

Once filled, take the piping bag out of the jug and squeeze all the buttercream down to the nozzle opening then twist the bag around the top of the buttercream. Hold this twist between your thumb and fingers.

Ready to pipe.

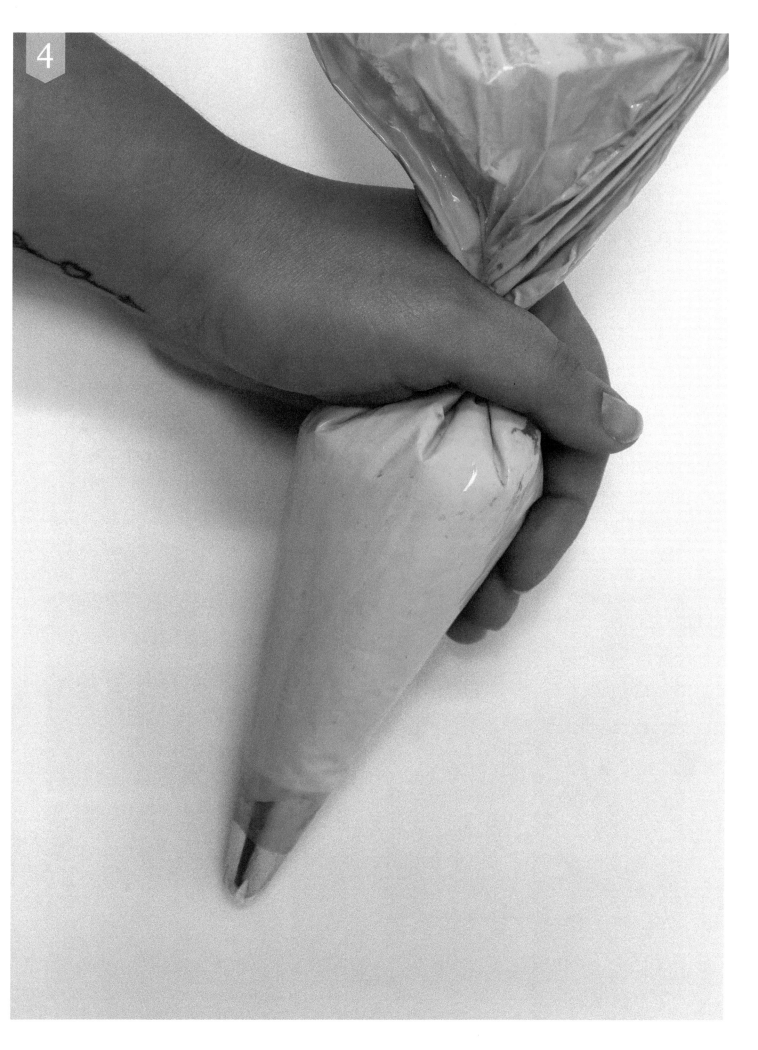

Some of my favourite piping techniques are here. You can use these methods on the top or side of cakes as shown later on in the book or on cupcakes. Play around with the nozzles too as they'll give different results. I've added my preferred nozzle for each method.

ROSE SWIRLS

Fill your piping bag with a Jem 2D nozzle and some lovely light fluffy buttercream.

Start by touching down to attach the buttercream then gently start squeezing. Make sure you don't rush. Go nice and steady.

You're going to begin in the middle and pipe a swirl going outwards.

Slowly move your hand around, squeezing out buttercream as you go, keeping that nice slow swirl...

Finally, when it's big enough, just stop squeezing and pull away gently.

Fill your piping bag with an Open star 172 nozzle and some yummy buttercream.

This one is super easy.

Squeeze a little buttercream out to attach it.

Keep your piping bag still but lift it up slightly and begin to squeeze buttercream out.

Once this piped shape is at the size you like, just stop squeezing and gently pull up to finish.

This shape is great for filling in gaps around other piping work.

RUFFLES

My favourite nozzle to pipe ruffles with is a Wilton 104. I use it for all ruffles on cakes and cupcakes.

It's important to use the nozzle the correct way around. It is shaped like a thin tear drop. Make sure the wider part of the tear drop is against the cake. The thinner tip of the tear drop should be the tip of the ruffle.

Start piping with the nozzle on a 90 degree angle to your cake. Gently start squeezing some buttercream out. Then just wiggle!!

And keep on wiggling back and forth to make a lovely line of ruffles. When you are done, stop squeezing and pull away.

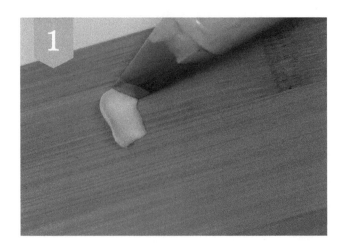

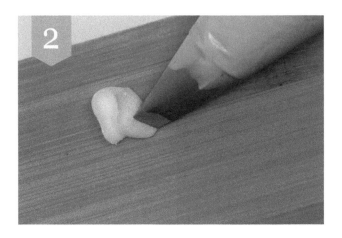

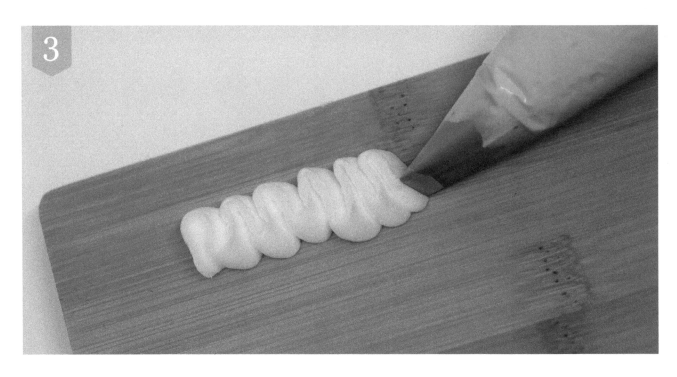

This is the best swirl.... fact! Perfect for the top of big cakes or loading up a cupcake. I use a Jem 2D nozzle for this one.

Squeeze a little buttercream out and touch down to attach it onto your cake or cupcake. You are going to pipe 3 circles, each sitting on top of another, each a little smaller than the one before. Pipe your first circle of buttercream.

Then continue piping your next circle on top of the first one.

Now pipe the last circle on top which should be the smallest. Stop squeezing and gently pull away.

Perfect to finish off with sprinkles.

Making rainbow buttercream or even just two tone buttercream can add such a fun element to your cakes and bakes. You'll be using this technique in my Pastel party cookie on page 116 and with my Mint chocolate chip cupcakes (Page 100) creating just 2 rows using mint green and chocolate buttercream.

First, mix up your buttercream colours using your chosen colours. I use Colour Mill for buttercream. These mix so well and don't leave any clumps of unmixed colour.

You wont need much buttercream per colour but obviously this depends on how many colours you want and what you are decorating.

Lay out a sheet of cling film. Using a spoon, place your coloured buttercream in rows.

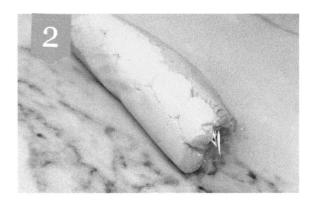

Roll up the cling film into a tube and snip off the end exposing the rows of buttercream. Now place this buttercream tube inside a piping bag.

Fold the piping bag back up over the cling film roll and twist around the top of the buttercream. Hold this twist in your fingers and thumb.

Pipe a small amount out first to test the colours. Make sure the colours are how you like before piping onto the cake.

Take your cooled cake and a cake leveller. Set the leveller to half way up the cake and begin to slice through the cake.

Ensure you keep both feet of the leveller flat on your work surface as you saw through the cake.

Pop a small amount of buttercream on a cake drum and spread out with a palette knife. Put your cake on this which will stick it down to the drum. Ensure the cake is central.

I like to add my buttercream in a piping bag to ensure an even layer. Or you can just spread on using a palette knife if you prefer.

Pipe a layer of buttercream over the surface of the cake.

Smooth out with your palette knife.

You can add other fillings if you wish, such as jam, chocolate sauce, toffee sauce, depending on your cake flavour.

Repeat the same steps with building up the rest of the cake

All done and ready to eat, decorate or add a crumbcoat.

If your cake is super tall or a little slippy from your fillings, I'd recommend to put a central dowel or straw through the middle of your cake and cut it level with the top. This will prevent the layers from moving and sliding when decorating and transporting.

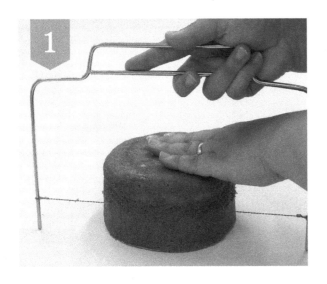
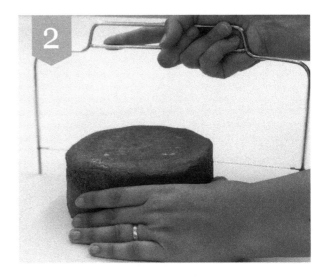

This is the basis for all cake decorating. Unless you are leaving it as a naked cake for example! A crumb coat will trap any crumbs in the buttercream. This will give a really neat, smooth finish to the cake and also leave a little cake showing through like on my Chocolate donut cake on page 68. This is the first stage to decorating before adding your final coat of buttercream.

Take some yummy buttercream and begin spreading this around the stacked cake using a palette knife.

Continue adding the buttercream all over the cake, filling in any gaps. It doesn't need to be smooth at this point. You just want a thick layer all over.

Ensure you've completely covered the cake not forgetting the top too.

Take a scraper, making sure this is taller than the cake and start to scrape off and smooth out the buttercream.

Ensure your scraper is clean at all times and just keep smoothing out the buttercream.

If there are any gaps, pop a little more buttercream on the cake and smooth again.

Once you can start to see some cake showing through the buttercream and there isn't much more to scrape off, you are done and this is perfect.

Just make sure it is a smooth as it can be.

Once the sides of the cake are smooth, hold your palette knife over the edge of the cake and pull back towards the middle to get lovely sharp edges to your buttercream.

Your cake is now ready to put in the fridge for 30-40 minutes. This is then ready for the next step or the perfect semi naked cake.

Once you've added your first crumbcoat and this has set in the fridge, next you need to cover the cake in a thick layer of buttercream. You can either use a palette knife to spread it over the cake or a piping bag of buttercream to pipe a layer all over.

Start by smoothing over the top of the cake with a palette knife and get this flat and level. You can push all the excess buttercream over the edge as this will help with achieving a nice sharp edge to your cake.

Take a side scraper and begin to smooth out the sides of the cake. You don't want to press too hard as this will scrape off the buttercream. Instead, focus on smoothing this out.

Continue around the cake until as smooth as possible.

Top tip - You can heat up the metal scraper in hot water and then smooth around the cake. This melts the very top layer of the buttercream to get the smoothest finish.

You can leave the top edge with this textured finish (such as on my Pink splatter cake page 92)

Or for a sharp smooth edge, hold your palette knife on the top, over the edge and smooth towards the middle.

You can put this cake in the fridge to firm up fully for at least 1 hour now before decorating.

Ganache is essentially a mix of chocolate and cream. The quantities of chocolate and cream depend on what chocolate you use and what you are using the ganache for. We're going to be making ganache for lovely drip cakes and below you'll find the quantities for this.

Start by weighing out and adding your ingredients into your bowl.

Dark Chocolate Drip Ganache -

50g Dark chocolate

50ml Cream

Pop this bowl in the microwave on high for 20 seconds then stir well.

Now pop on high again for another 15 seconds then stir until melted.

If it hasn't completely melted after this, microwave again for 5-10 seconds and stir until melted.

There is such a small amount of

YOU'LL NEED

Chocolate -
I always use Callebaut chocolate pellets as it's such good quality and makes the best ganache in my opinion.

Scales

Double cream - I always use Elmlea.

A microwave safe bowl

cream here that it gets really hot quickly. However, you don't want to boil the cream for a few reasons. Firstly, it will split the cream and chocolate. It will start to separate and the oils from the chocolate will start to show. This is no good for drips and you'll need to start again if this happens. Secondly, if the ganache is too hot, it'll melt the cake. Especially if it's a buttercream cake you are dripping on to. It should be smooth and silky looking, like this.

Now, you are ready to pour into a piping bag and drip away!

White Chocolate Drip Ganache

60g White Chocolate

40ml Cream

Milk Chocolate Drip Ganache

50g milk chocolate

40ml cream

The method for making all ganache for drips is the same as above. Make sure you take into account your own microwave and heat up according to your instructions. If using fresh cream, ensure this is heated to almost boiling before adding the chocolate separately then stirring until melted.

I use a simple sugar syrup on all my cakes. This is a mix of caster sugar and water to create a thick syrup which is then brushed over the cake layers. It helps keep the cake fresh and moist for a little longer.

Mix together 60g of caster sugar and 60ml of boiling water. Stir these together until completely melted. This should be thick like maple syrup now.

Take a silicone brush and brush over your layered cakes before stacking.

INGREDIENTS

200g granulated sugar

100g salted butter

110mls thick double cream

2-3 tsp salt

This delicious caramel recipe is really to make. Use it to layer in your big cakes, to fill your cupcakes, to drizzle over buttercream or just grab a spoon and dig in!

Get all your ingredients prepared before starting. Chop the butter up into chunks. and measure out the cream.

Begin by heating the sugar in a saucepan over a low - medium heat. It's best to take your time doing this. Make sure you stir this constantly. The sugar will go quite lumpy then turn an amber/brown colour. It can burn very easily now.

Next, add the butter chunks and keep stirring. Make sure this is on the lowest heat. It may bubble but keep continually stirring. Once the butter is all melted add the salt and pour in the cream slowly. It will bubble lots but again, keep stirring. Boil for 45 seconds then remove from the heat and allow to cool before use.

Perfect and really easy salted caramel. Store in the fridge and use to fill or drizzle over your cakes.

CAKE RECIPES AND DECORATING

This cake is a simple one but really tasty. All cakes do not need to be covered and overly detailed. Sometimes, just some simple jam, buttercream in the layers and topped with fresh edible flowers and fruit is enough. Simple ingredients and easy to bake. I've been baking this recipe for years and it's always my go to bake.

PREPARATION

Preparation Time
15 Minutes

Baking Time
40 Minutes

Decorating Time
30 Minutes

Serves
12-15 Portions

Preheat oven to
160 Fan

INGREDIENTS

350g self raising flour

350g caster sugar

350g unsalted butter

7 medium eggs

2 tsp vanilla extract

Pop all your ingredients in a mixer. Yes, ALL of it together. And mix until combined. (I told you it was easy!)

Put your batter equally in 2 lined cake tins and in a preheated fan oven at 160 for 40 mins or until cooked. For a softer bake, try cooking in 4 cake tins for 30 minutes.

Keep in the tins for 15-20 minutes to cool, turn the cake out on to a wire rack to cool further.

Once completely cooled, take a leveller and level your cakes leaving you with 4 layers of cake. Stack up using buttercream and any other filling you like (jam is delicious!!)

I topped this simple cake with edible flowers from Greens of Devon and some fresh strawberries and cherries.

Why not jazz it up a little and add in some sprinkles for a funfetti cake. Take a look at the confetti sprinkles from @icedjems which are perfect for this. Use 120g of sprinkles in this recipe and stir in by hand at the end.

If you want to spruce up the fresh vanilla cake with a little more pizzazz, take a look at this one. Vanilla cake but this time covered in a smooth coating of buttercream, finished with perfect drips and vibrant sprinkles.

I'd recommend decorating the day after baking. Just wrap the cooled cake in cling film and store at room temp for 24 hours. The cake is really soft when first baked which makes this kind of decorating tricky. Leaving the cake to settle will make this decorating much easier.

Begin by adding a crumb coat (as shown in page 48) and then your second crumb coat of your final cake colour (as shown in page 50)

First, let's make white chocolate ganache drips...

In a microwavable bowl add 60g of good quality white chocolate and 40ml of double cream. Microwave this for 20 seconds then stir. Then microwave again for 10 second intervals until just about melted. If you can still see small lumps of chocolate here thats fine. Just stir really well. The heat from the cream and chocolate mix will melt the remaining chocolate. If you over heat it in the microwave, it'll be too hot to put on the cake and melt the buttercream.

Once melted, add in a quarter teaspoon of food whitener. I use Wilton White White Icing Whitener. This will take the yellow tones out of the ganache drips which will make the end colour better.

1. Mix this well until an off white colour has been achieved.

2. You can now add your colour. I used Colour Mill Pink. Just keep adding colour until you are happy with the shade.

3. Put a piping bag into a glass or tub and fold over the rim. This helps keep the bag open. Pour the ganache into the piping bag.

4. Twist the piping bag above the ganache and hold securely in your hand.

Snip a small amount off the end of the piping bag and hold this in the middle on top of the cake. Careful as it will start to leak out as soon as you snip.

5. Now, hold over the edge of the cake and gently begin to squeeze a small pea size amount over the edge.

   The more ganache you squeeze over the edge, the longer your drips will be. There is no rush with this, take your time. This way you'll get a feel for how much to squeeze and how long the drips will be.

6. Continue around the cake adding your drips. Then squeeze out some ganache on to the top of the cake.

   Spread this out using a palette knife to the edge.

   You can pop this in the fridge for 10-15 minutes to help the drips set.

7. I used some bright star sprinkles to decorate this cake. Use some cake tweezers to pick up and press the star into the buttercream at the base of each drip. You could use any shape. Hearts would look really cute too!

   Next, add some sprinkles around the base of the cake. Use a palette knife to lift up some sprinkles and press them gently into the buttercream around the cake.

   You can place some of the larger sprinkles where you want them after.

8. Lastly, it's time to decorate the top. Fill a piping bag with buttercream (see page 38) with a Jem 2D nozzle and pipe some tall classic swirls. You can find more about piping techniques on page 40.

   Finish off with pretty sprinkles that match the bottom.

GORGEOUS OR WHAT!

Experiment with colours.. How about pale blue buttercream, green drips and mermaid sprinkles for a beach theme party cake. Or make this cake using a pink and blue theme for a gender reveal celebration.

PREPARATION

Preparation Time
15 Minutes

Baking Time
40 Minutes

Decorating Time
1 hour

Serves
12-15 Portions

Preheat oven to
160 Fan

INGREDIENTS

350g self raising flour

50g cocoa powder

2 tsp bicarbonate of soda

0.5 tsp baking powder

160g caster sugar

160g brown sugar

50g golden syrup

7 medium eggs, lightly beaten

200ml sunflower oil

2tsp vanilla extract

200ml whole milk

100g melted milk chocolate

This cake is super indulgent, moist and extra tasty. Full of chocolate flavour makes it perfect for a chocolate lover. This is a tall cake recipe. No point having a tiny chocolate cake. Once baked, layered and stacked you should have a 5-6 inch deep cake. Yum Yum!

In a mixer, add in all your dry ingredients. This is the flour, cocoa powder, both sugars, bicarb, baking powder. Once all in a bowl, mix together to combine.

In a separate bowl combine together all your wet ingredients. This is the eggs, vanilla, golden syrup, oil and milk. Lightly whisk together.

Add this wet mixture into your dry mixture and mix together until just combined.

Lastly, melt your chocolate in the microwave for a 30 second burst then stir. Pop on for another 20-30 second burst and stir until melted. Pour this into your cake batter and mix lightly. Pop into 2 lined baking tins and place into the oven at 160 for 40 mins or until cooked.

If cooking in more than 2 tins, reduce cooking time by 10 minutes. Always ensure the cake is cooked through.

Once cooked, leave to cool in the tins for 2 minutes then take out to cool further on a wire rack.

Level your cakes and then brush over with some sugar syrup to keep extra moist.

Stack up with some fresh vanilla buttercream and chocolate ganache in each layer. Yum Yum!

Begin by levelling, stacking and adding a crumb coat to your cake as shown on page 46.

Make up some dark chocolate ganache using 40g of dark chocolate and 40ml of cream. Heat together in the microwave for 30 seconds, staring half way through. Stir until melted.

Pop in a piping bag and snip the end off.

Slowly drip the ganache over the edge of your cake. Hold the piping bag very still and squeeze gently until a pea size amount has come out.

Continue around the cake, varying how much you squeeze out so the drips vary in length.

On this cake I added drips to 3/4 of the cake and left one section free of drips.

Squeeze a little more over the top and spread out with a palette knife

Put some chocolate buttercream in a piping bag with an open star tip and gently squeeze out. Then stop squeezing and lift up. Continue this piping around the ganache on the top.

Take some yummy chocolate covered donuts (as shown on page 126) add a cocktail stick half way into the donut to allow it to stand upright on the cake.

You can also cut a donut in half and add this on to the cake too. The other half is perfect for taste testing!!

Leave plain or finish the cake off with chocolate sprinkles.

PREPARATION

Preparation Time
20 Minutes

Baking Time
40 Minutes

Decorating Time
1 hour 30 Minutes

Serves
12-15 Portions

Preheat oven to
160 Fan

INGREDIENTS

350g plain flour

30g of cocoa

2 teaspoons of baking powder

320g caster sugar

200g salted butter

6 medium eggs

4 teaspoons of vanilla extract

200ml buttermilk

2-4 tsp of red food colouring (Sugarflair red extra)

Cream cheese frosting

150g unsalted butter

100g cream cheese

500g icing sugar

1/4 lemon juice

Red velvet cake is the most gorgeous deep red, smooth velvet cake with rich butter, vanilla, and cocoa flavours. This recipe is really easy and fuss free producing great vibrant results every time.

In your mixing bowl add in all your dry ingredients. This is your flour, cocoa, sugar and baking powder. Mix up to combine.

Meanwhile, pop your butter in the microwave to soften. It needs to be able to mix easily with the other ingredients. Normally around 30 seconds for this amount of butter straight from the fridge should be fine.

In a separate bowl, whisk up all the wet ingredients. This is the eggs, buttermilk, vanilla and butter. (Don't worry about what this looks like!)

Add this to your dry mixture. Mix together on high until just combined.

Lastly add in your red food colouring and mix well. How much you add is up to you. Make sure you use the most concentrated colour you can find. I use Red Extra food colouring from Sugar Flair. It produces a really rich red colour.

Add the batter into 2 lined tins and bake for 40 minutes or until cooked.

If baking in more than 2 tins, reduce the cooking time by 10 minutes.

Once baked, turn out on to a cooling rack after 15 minutes in the tin and allow to cool completely.

Next, layer your cakes. I use a cake leveller for this. It makes the job so much easier. Then brush on your sugar syrup to each layer. This just helps to keep the cake moist for a little longer.

Now you can stack using your delicious fillings - see page 46.

Start with a crumb coated cake thats been chilled in the fridge and then add a thick, final layer of buttercream on to this. There is no need to refrigerate again. Just move straight on to these steps below.

Add a row of pink buttercream around the base of the cake using your palette knife.

Then add a row of cream above this which will blend the colours together as you smooth it out.

Warm up your scraper in some hot water then smooth out this buttercream.

This slightly melts the top layer of buttercream giving you a much smoother result.

Make sure the top of the cake is sharp and flat using your palette knife. Drag it from the outside edge into the middle.

Keep going until smooth all over then pop in the fridge for 30 minutes to set.

Mix up some 2 tone buttercream using the method on page 44 I used plain and pink buttercream

coloured using Colour Mill hot pink.

I used a Jem 2D Nozzle for this piping.

Start by adding some flat rose swirls to the side of your cake.

Continue adding the swirls until you are happy with the end result.

Next take an open star nozzle and pipe on some stars to the cake. I used more of the 2 tone colour here.

Mix up some dark pink buttercream using sugar flair red extra and add this into a piping bag with a small open star nozzle. Pipe some extra dark pink detail on this cake.

You can continue to add piping around the top of the cake too.

Finish off with some sprinkles. I used sprinkles from @super_streusel and @sweet.stamp

I've teamed this delicious coffee flavour cake with my jungle design (page 78) because the brown tint of the sponge matches the theme of the cake really well. Obviously mix and match flavours with designs to suit you. Try playing with the colours of buttercream fillings for this cake, maybe add some shades of green buttercream in the layers to produce a great effect when you slice this jungle cake open.

PREPARATION

Preparation Time
20 Minutes

Baking Time
40 Minutes

Decorating Time
1 hour 30 Minutes

Serves
12-15 Portions

Preheat oven to
160 Fan

INGREDIENTS

370g self-raising flour

170g light brown sugar

170g dark muscovado sugar

250g salted butter

6 eggs

120 ml whole milk

4-5 tsp instant coffee

3 tsp vanilla extract

Weigh out both of the sugars and the butter. Make sure the butter has been softened in a microwave, but not melted. Mix these together for around 2-3 minutes.

While this is mixing, measure out the milk and coffee. Pop this in a microwave for 20 - 30 seconds until the coffee has just started to melt. The milk doesn't need to be heated too much. Mix this up until smooth as you don't want any lumps of coffee in your batter. Add in your vanilla and stir.

Now, in your butter/sugar mix, add in an egg at a time alternating with a spoon full of flour until all those ingredients are in and the batter is combined well.

Pour the coffee mixture in the batter and stir slowly until just combined then stop mixing.

Pop in 2 lined tins and the into the oven for 40 minutes or until a skewer comes out clean. Leave to cool.

If cooking in more than 2 tins, reduce the cooking time by 10 minutes. Ensure the cake is cooked before removing from the oven.

Once cool, brush on sugar syrup to your layered cakes.

This cake is full of character and charm. Especially when topped with the gorgeous jungle party animals from Cake Topper Animals. You can have real fun with the stencilling and piping. Less is not more on this cake!

To start, complete your cake with a smooth coat of buttercream. Ensure your cake is completely set and firm. I'd recommend popping the cake in the freezer for 10 minutes before the stencilling.

Take a leaf stencil.

Mix up some green buttercream. Here I made 2 different shade of green using Colour Mill mint green and emerald green.

Take your leaf stencil and hold against the cake.

Take a palette knife and a small amount of buttercream and lightly spread this over part of the stencil.

Repeat this with the second colour buttercream on the remaining parts of the stencil until covered. Make sure this buttercream is not thick and you've scraped off excess.

Remove the stencil away from the cake and you'll be left with a leaf shape on the cake.

You'll have to wash the leaf stencil before adding the next leaf on or you'll put buttercream back on the

cake in places where you don't want it.

Continue around the cake adding as many leaves as you like.

Top Tip - If you feel like the cake is melting as you hold the stencil on the cake, pop back in the freezer for just a few minutes to firm up again.

Next, let's paint the leopard print.

I use Sweet Sticks Paint. These are edible paints ready to use from the pot which makes cake life so much easier.

I used a mix of peach and brown to create different shades of brown. Then black for the outside of the shape.

Make sure your cake is set completely before painting.

Start off with the brown paint and a number 2 brush. Add a little paint on your brush at a time. Paint a brown splodge on the cake. It doesn't need to be perfect, just a wobbly circle shape. The less perfect the shape is, the better it will look. Vary these shapes in size.

Next take some black paint and paint curved lines around the brown shapes. You can go all the way around or just add a few lines. This is up to you. Just vary the lines you paint.

Continue around the cake adding as much painting as you like.

Next, have some fun with your piping!

Create swirls, stars and ruffles on this fun cake.

Once you've completed this you can finish off the cake design with some fun accessories.

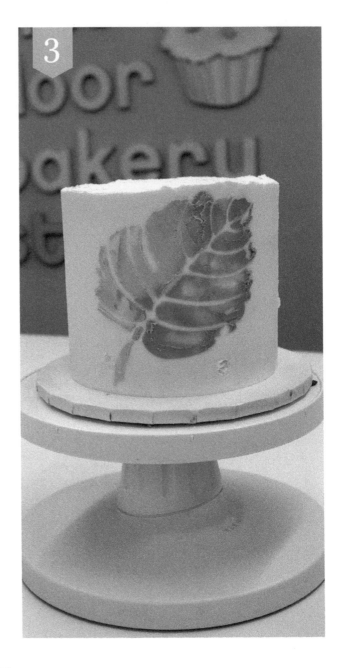

INGREDIENTS

For the tray bake:

8 x 8 inch square tin

240g self-raising flour

0.5 tsp baking powder

100g caster sugar

100g brown sugar

50ml vegetable oil

70ml whole milk

120g melted butter

3 medium eggs

2 tsp vanilla extract

70ml sour cream

100g crushed Oreos, you can leave them chunky!

For the frosting:

75g cream cheese

250g icing sugar

100g butter

1 pack crushed Oreos to top

100g crushed Oreos, you can leave them chunky!

This cake is so delicious, sweet and definitely a firm favourite in my house. This is a tasty tray bake which is perfect for a quick bake in the morning before a lunch time date. I've also included a 6inch round cake recipe too. Best of both worlds.

PREPARATION

Preparation Time
15 Minutes

Baking Time
30-40 Minutes

Decorating Time
20-30 Minutes

Serves
16 Portions

Preheat oven to
160 Fan

Pre-heat your oven to 160C and line a square tin (8 x 8 inch) with baking paper.

Make your cake batter using the all in one method (leaving out the Oreos). Simply add all the ingredients into your mixer and combine all the ingredients together until lump free.

Once your batter is smooth and mixed through, add in some crushed Oreos, and fold in by hand using spatula. I like to leave these oreos chunky but you can crush them as much as you like.

Pour the batter into the prepared tin and bake for 30-40 minutes or until cooked through.

While the cake cools, make the frosting.

To start, make sure your butter is softened. Put the butter in a stand mixer with a paddle attachment and mix until it goes light and fluffy. Then add in the icing sugar and mix thoroughly. Add in about 5-6 crushed oreos and the cream cheese and mix until just combined. Don't over do this bit.

Once the cake is cool, spread on the frosting using a palette knife (as thick as you like) and sprinkle a generous helping of crushed Oreos on top.

VARIATIONS

For a 6 inch round cake use this recipe with the same method as above. Bake in 2 tins for around 40 mins or until cooked. Yum YUM! If baking in more tins, reduce the cooking time for 10 minutes.

350g self-raising flour	80ml vegetable oil	3 tsp vanilla extract
1 tsp baking powder	120ml whole milk	100ml sour cream
150g caster sugar	180g melted butter	150g crushed Oreos,
150g brown sugar	5 medium eggs	you can leave them chunky!

PREPARATION

Preparation Time
20 Minutes

Baking Time
60 Minutes

Decorating Time
10 Minutes

Serves
10-12 Slices

Preheat oven to
140 Fan

INGREDIENTS

225g self raising flour

225g caster sugar

225g butter

4 eggs

Juice of 1 lemon

1 tsp lemon extract

Zest of 3-4 medium lemons

Crunchy glaze drizzle

80g caster sugar

juice from 1 lemon

Smooth drizzle

3 tbsp icing sugar

My mums lemon drizzle cake is my favourite ever. It is so zesty as in my opinion there is no point having a lemon cake that barely tastes of lemons. And it lasts for ages too! Absolutely delicious. Its cooked on a low temp and really slow for the yummiest bake.

Cream together the butter and sugar until really light and fluffy. Make sure you scrape down the mixing bowl half way through to ensure it's all mixed up really well.

Add in 1 egg followed by 1 spoon of flour and mix. Keep this method up until all the flour and eggs have been added. Next you can add in all the flavouring. So squeeze your lemon, zest the lemons and pop in your extract and mix through for 20-30 seconds.

Line a 2lb loaf tin with baking paper and pop the batter in. Put in a pre heated oven for at least 50 minutes before checking to see if it's cooked.

Now, for the glaze. You can either make a smooth or a crunchy glaze. I love the crunchy glaze. It works perfectly with the cake.

Add the ingredients into a bowl and mix through. When the cake is cooked and still in the loaf tin and still warm, poke holes in the top of the cake using a skewer and pour over the glaze slowly so the drizzle sinks into the cake. Leave the cool then turn out. Mix up 2 tbsp of royal icing powder and a few drops of water until at a thick consistency that pours well. Add this into a piping bag. Finish off with royal icing drizzle and lemon slices across the top.

Start by preparing your cake in the stages previously shown and finish off with a gorgeous coat of smooth blue buttercream. I used Sugarflair colour Ice Blue.

Now time for the sprinkles. I used a gorgeous sprinkle mix from @super_streusel.

Using your hand gently add some sprinkles around the base of your cake.

Then take a palette knife and scoop some up.

Then lift this onto the cake and gently press into the buttercream.

I'd recommend sticking to smaller sprinkles here then you can add in any larger ones afterwards.

Next, take a glass of water. Dip the tip of your finger in the water (you can take off the excess water by blotting on some kitchen roll) then take your damp finger and press into some sprinkles. The wet will stick sprinkles to your finger enabling you to press these into the buttercream with ease.

Finish off with some pink buttercream classic swirls and matching sprinkles on top.

Add a thick, even layer of chocolate buttercream to your cake

Take a stripe scraper. I use @finchbakery medium scraper here.

Start to scrape off your buttercream keeping the scraper as straight as possible.

Add more buttercream in any gaps you have and scrape again.

You need to make sure the stripes are as full and straight as possible.

Hold your palette knife flat on the top of the cake over the edge and drag into the middle of the cake lifting away any excess.

Once you are happy, pop the cake in the fridge for an hour or the freezer for 10 minutes to set.

Fill up a piping bag with your remaining chocolate buttercream and pipe into the top few stripe spaces. Make sure you have slightly over filled them.

Make some darker chocolate buttercream, either with more cocoa powder or add some dark brown food colouring.

Add into a piping bag and pipe around the bottom few empty stripes.

Using the straight side of the scraper,

you can now start to scrape away the excess and blend the stripes together.

Keep smoothing out. Make sure you keep your scraper clean of buttercream after every scrape.

It will help to heat up your scraper in some hot water and smooth out the buttercream at the end which will produce a really smooth finish to your cake.

Finish off with some dark chocolate ganache drips and buttercream swirls.

I made the small chocolate bars on top using a mini chocolate bar mould. Put a hand full of dark chocolate in a microwave bowl and heat for 30 seconds. Stir until this is melted. Spread into the mould until full then scrape away all the excess.

Put in the freezer for 10 minutes to set.

Lastly, pop out these little chocolate bars and stick into the buttercream swirls.

Enjoy!

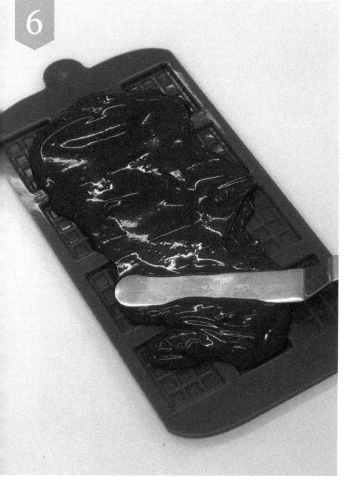

This is a really fun, abstract cake which is perfect for parties, celebrations or even quirky wedding cakes. Try varying the colours. How about a rainbow version and covered in rainbow sprinkles! Cake Dreams!! Get creative with this cake and I'd love to see your versions. Tag me @bluedoorbakery

Start with your set, smooth buttercream cake.

Mix up a small amount of pink buttercream. I used Colour Mill Pink here.

Make sure your cake has been in the fridge for at least 30 minutes.

Add small blobs of pink buttercream to the cake. Don't make them too big as they'll end up bigger once you've smoothed them out.

Smooth them out a few at a time then clean off your scraper. If there is buttercream still on your scraper, this will then go back on the cake

when you smooth the next one so ensure you've wiped off any buttercream on your scraper.

Then mix up a slightly darker shade of pink and repeat the same process.

For the paint splatter I use sweet sticks edible paint. Pop a small amount on a paintbrush and holding your finger behind the brush, flick this on to create paint splatter all over the cake.

Top tip - You can pop the cake inside a cardboard box to help with the splatter mess!

I use matching sprinkles to add the final touch to the cake. Just gently press these into the cake. Not too far or they'll sink right into the buttercream.

Lastly, pop back in the fridge for an hour to firm up.

CUPCAKES

PINK LEMONADE CUPCAKES

PREPARATION

Preparation Time
15 Minutes

Baking Time
20 Minutes

Decorating Time
30 Minutes

Serves
12 Cupcakes

Preheat oven to
170 Fan

INGREDIENTS

225g self raising flour

125g butter, softened

225g caster sugar

3 medium eggs

120ml milk

Zest and juice of 1 lemon

1tsp lemon extract

Yellow food colouring
 (optional)

Raspberry buttercream

70g raspberries

Juice of ½ a lemon

150g unsalted butter, softened

450g icing sugar

Plus

Fresh raspberries, zest of 1
 lemon and coloured paper
 straws to decorate

Cream together the butter and sugar until pale and fluffy, about 2-3 minutes. Add in the eggs, one at a time. Followed by the milk, lemon juice, extract and lemon zest.

Next, add in the flour and mix until combined.

Optional step - add in a small pea size amount of yellow food colour.

Add the cupcake batter into cases using a 56mm ice cream scoop and bake for 15-20 minutes, or until the cakes are risen, golden and a skewer inserted comes out clean.

To make the raspberry buttercream, put the raspberries in a bowl and using a fork, mash up until really crushed and small. You could also use a food processor for this (or a nutribullet like I do!) Add the juice of half a lemon.

Mix the butter until light and fluffy then add in icing sugar. Add in the raspberry mush (thats the official name for this!) until it is all incorporated. If the mixture looks split, add a few tablespoons more of icing sugar and mix really well until it comes back together and looks smooth. You can add a little pink food colouring if you like more of a richer colour.

Fill a piping bag with a Jem 2D nozzle and pipe lovely huge classic swirls on your cooled cupcakes. Top each cupcake with a fresh raspberry or lemon slice and paper straw.

MINT CHOCOLATE CHIP CUPCAKES

PREPARATION

Preparation Time
15 Minutes

Baking Time
20 Minutes

Decorating Time
30 Minutes

Serves
12 Cupcakes

Preheat oven to
160 Fan

INGREDIENTS

200g self raising flour

225g salted butter

225g caster sugar

3 eggs

30g cocoa powder

50ml condensed milk

1 tsp peppermint extract

Mint chocolate aero bubbles

Buttercream

200g unsalted butter

400g icing sugar

Sugarflair party green
  food colouring

Peppermint extract

These delicious cupcakes have an amazing flavour. The rich chocolate with a hint of mint and the hidden surprise in the centre makes these cupcakes a real winner.

Before you start, pop your aero bubbles in the freezer. Begin by creaming the butter and sugar together. Meanwhile, weigh out the flour and cocoa powder together in a separate bowl.

In a jug, add in the condensed milk, eggs and peppermint extract and gently whisk. Add this into the butter mixture, give the bowl a scrape down and mix.

Next spoon in the flour and cocoa and mix until all is combined.

Using an ice cream scoop, add this batter into your cupcake cases. Before they head into the oven, put a mint chocolate aero bubble into the batter. Place it on top and then push down into the batter until level with the top. Cook on 160 for 18 minutes then turn the trays around and cook for a further 2-3 minutes.

Make the buttercream without the flavouring and colour at this point. Take half the buttercream in a bowl. Add in some mint green food colouring and 1tsp of peppermint extract and mix. With the other half of the buttercream, add in a tbsp of cocoa powder and mix through.

Create two tone piping using the methods on page 44 and use a large open star 172 nozzle.

Pipe some gorgeous tall classic swirls and sprinkle with chocolate sprinkles.

PREPARATION

Preparation Time
15 Minutes

Baking Time
20 Minutes

Decorating Time
30 Minutes

Serves
12 Cupcakes

Preheat oven to
170 Fan

INGREDIENTS

225g self raising flour

225g unsalted butter

225g golden caster sugar

4 eggs

1 large tbsp. black treacle

2 tbsp golden syrup

Buttercream

200g unsalted butter

400g icing sugar

1 tsp vanilla extract

This is one of my best cupcake recipes. It is so delicious and easily one of my most requested cupcakes to take to family and friends.

Cream the butter and sugar together for a few minutes. It should look pale, light and fluffy. Next, add 1 egg at a time until combined. Don't worry if it looks scrambled!

Scrape down your mixing bowl then add a spoonful of flour at a time. Finally, add in your black treacle and golden syrup.

Mix for 20 seconds on high at the end to mix it all together.

Use your ice cream scoop to put the batter into the cupcake cases and bake for around 20 minutes or until cooked.

Make some delicious vanilla buttercream. Using an open star nozzle in a piping bag, pipe some rose swirls on top of the cupcake. Add some salted caramel into a piping bag and drizzle over the top. Finish off with fudge pieces.

Top Tip - Why not pipe some salted caramel sauce into the sponge cake too? Poke a hole in the cake using a skewer then pipe a some sauce into this before piping with buttercream.

BANANA AND CARAMEL CUPCAKES

PREPARATION

Preparation Time
15 Minutes

Baking Time
20 Minutes

Decorating Time
30 Minutes

Serves
12 Cupcakes

Preheat oven to
170 Fan

INGREDIENTS

220g plain flour

1.5 tsp baking powder

150g light soft brown sugar

50g caster sugar

2 medium mashed bananas

3 tbsp golden syrup

3 medium eggs

200g unsalted butter
    (melted)

Buttercream

150g unsalted butter

400g icing sugar

1 tbsp caramel

1 banana mush

Make these easy and super delicious banana cupcakes from start to finish in just 35 minutes. Perfect for picnics, parties or whenever you fancy a sweet bake. With the addition of a caramel drizzle too, they'll be a hit every time.

Start by mixing the butter and sugars together until light and creamy. Add in eggs and golden syrup and mix up for 30 seconds. Squish up your banana using a fork and add in this to the mixture.

Next, add in the flour and baking powder and beat until combined well.

Pop into cupcake cases using the 56mm scoop and cook in a preheated oven for 20 minutes, turn the trays around and bake for a further 2-3 minutes.

Once baked, allow to cool in the muffin trays. Meanwhile make the buttercream.

Mix the butter on high until pale and fluffy. Scrape down the bowl then add in your icing sugar. The icing sugar to butter ratio is high in this recipe as with the addition of the caramel and banana it can make the buttercream quite sloppy. So you need the extra icing sugar to stabilise it. Add in the caramel and mashed banana and mix. Then pop this buttercream in the fridge for 5-10 minutes. It really helps to keep it firm before piping.

Place an open nozzle into a piping bag and add in some buttercream. Pipe one circle around then pipe another circle on top which is the same size.

If you fancy making your own caramel… take a look at page 56 it's really easy!! If you don't want to make your own, you can purchase all kinds of ready made and tasty caramel from supermarkets now.

Fill the buttercream central hole (if you have one) with some caramel. Place a banana slice on top then drizzle with more caramel to finish. I also topped with a sprinkling of chocolate.

Top tip - Sometimes if the buttercream is a little soft, it can squish the first buttercream circle. If that happens, pipe your first circle then pop the cupcakes in the fridge for 10 minutes to firm this buttercream before piping your second circle.

How about using the same recipe above and put in a lined loaf tin, cook for 40-50 minutes or until cooked for a delicious banana loaf.

This recipe makes 12 delicious Vanilla cupcakes. It's my go to recipe. It's a foolproof recipe for perfect cupcakes every time.

PREPARATION

Preparation Time
15 Minutes

Baking Time
20 Minutes

Decorating Time
30 Minutes

Serves
12 Cupcakes

Preheat oven to
170 Fan

INGREDIENTS

210g caster sugar

60g unsalted butter

190g self raising flour

2 eggs

180g whole milk

1tsp vanilla extract

Buttercream

250g unsalted butter

500g icing sugar

1tsp vanilla extract

Mix up the butter and sugar in your mixer. Stop and wipe any mixture from the side of the bowl, then continue to mix for a few minutes.

Weigh out and add in the flour to the bowl of butter and sugar and mix until it resembles a fine breadcrumb.

In a jug, weigh out your milk (yes, weigh it! A weight measurement of ml and g are pretty similar anyway) Also add in your eggs and vanilla, and lightly whisk up.

Scrape down the mixing bowl and ensure nothing is stuck to the bowl then on a slow speed, pour in the milk mixture and mix through until just combined. It forms a smooth batter.

Make sure you keep it on slow and stop as soon as it's just combined. You can finish off mixing by hand with a spatula if needed. It's really easy to over mix this batter. This can mean that you end up with a dense cake. No one wants that!

Scoop in your cupcake cases.

Bake at 170 C for 18 minutes. Then turn the cakes around and bake for a further 2 minutes. Times will vary up to 5 minutes either way depending on your oven.

The cakes are cooked when they are pale golden and when you touch the top they feel slightly springy.

Make some delicious buttercream. Don't forget to add a little boiling water at the end to make it light and fluffy. Put a Jem 2D nozzle in a piping bag and fill with buttercream. Then pipe lovely tall classic swirls.

Lastly, finish off with a rainbow sprinkle selection and sprinkle away!

Make sure you sprinkle as soon as you've piped each cupcake. If you sprinkle after, the buttercream dries a little and some of the sprinkles won't stick as well.

Why not pipe some strawberry jam into the cupcake before piping for a tasty twist.

PREPARATION

Preparation Time
15 Minutes

Baking Time
20 Minutes

Decorating Time
30 Minutes

Serves
12 Cupcakes

Preheat oven to
170 Fan

INGREDIENTS

160g self raising flour

30g cocoa

210g caster sugar

60g unsalted butter

2 eggs

110ml whole milk

60ml condensed milk

1tsp vanilla extract

Buttercream

250g salted butter

500g icing sugar

2 tbsp cocoa powder

Ganache

30ml double cream

30ml dark chocolate

These cupcakes are so rich and decadent. They make the best mid afternoon treat! Get these baked, make a cuppa, put your feet up and enjoy!

Mix together your butter and sugar until fine and grainy. Add in the flour and cocoa and mix until this resembles bread crumbs. Scrape down your mixing bowl before the next stage.

In a jug mix together the milk, condensed milk, eggs and vanilla. Lightly whisk this then add into your flour mixture. Mix on a slow speed until you've poured in all the milky mixture then stop mixing. Move on to mixing this by hand with a spatula to ensure it is not over mixed.

Scoop into cupcake cases and bake for 18 minutes, turn the trays around and bake for a further 2-3 minutes.

Next, make up some chocolate buttercream. Add this delicious buttercream into a piping bag with a nozzle of your choosing. Here I picked an open star nozzle and pipe a small classic swirl.

Also make some chocolate ganache. Add the cream and chocolate in a bowl and microwave for 30 seconds. Stir this until it's melted then put in a piping bag. Snip the end off and drizzle over the top. Pile high some marshmallows and lightly brown with a blow torch. Be careful not to touch the ganache or buttercream or it'll make it a little soft and mushy.

Top tip - To make these extra yummy, how about piping some chocolate ganache into the cupcake before piping with buttercream. Just poke a hole in the cake using a skewer and pipe some in.

COOKIES

TRIPLE CHOCOLATE COOKIES

These cookies are beyond tasty. Full of flavour and even better the day after. They take on a tacky chocolate texture and are utterly devine.

Chill time: these cookies must be chilled or they spread out too much when cooking so plan accordingly.

PREPARATION

Makes
18-20 Cookies

Preheat oven to
170 Fan

INGREDIENTS

125g unsalted butter (make sure this is really soft)

95g brown soft sugar

95g dark brown sugar

2 tsp vanilla extract

1 medium free-range egg, beaten

195g plain flour

3 tbsp cocoa powder

1 tsp baking powder

3 tbsp golden syrup

80g milk chocolate chips

80g white chocolate chips

Put everything in the mixer apart from all the chocolate chips. Mix together on high for around 30 seconds. Add in the chocolate chips and mix through by hand.

Line a tray with baking paper. Using your 56mm ice cream scoop, fill with cookie dough and press out on to the baking paper. Once you've got your balls of dough, pop these in the freezer for 10-15 minutes or the fridge for 1 hour.

Once set, cook for 10-11 minutes.

The cookies will feel very soft and squidgy when they come out the oven. However as they cool, they will firm up so don't move them off the tray until completely cool. (although feel free to eat one while still soft and warm, this is one of life's simple pleasures and should be enjoyed to the full!!)

Variations - Make it a more indulgent cookie by using 50g each of dark, milk or white chips.

These cookies will keep for 5-6 days stored in a cake tin or air tight container.

PREPARATION

Makes
18-20 Cookies

Preheat oven to
150 Fan

INGREDIENTS

110g sugar

350g plain flour

225g butter

To decorate -

100-150g of white
  chocolate

Royal icing

Spinkles

Chop the butter into small pieces and rub together with the flour in a mixing bowl until you get small crumbs which resembles bread crumbs.

Add the sugar to the bowl and mix it together to make a dough.

Wrap the dough in clingfilm and place in the fridge for 30 minutes.

Once chilled, roll out until they are approx 1cm thick and cut out into shapes. Place on lined baking tray.

Bake in the pre-heated oven. Check after 6 minutes and cook 7-10 minutes. Keep checking to make sure they don't overcook, all ovens can be different. They are cooked when they are just starting to turn very light brown on the edges. They will firm up once cooled.

Once cooked, place to cool on a wire rack.

Once cool, you can now decorate. Melt your white chocolate in a microwave on 15-20 second bursts until melted. Next, add in a colour. I'd highly recommend using colour mill for colouring chocolate. I used pink.

Holding one corner of your shortbread, dip

half the biscuit in the chocolate and allow the excess to drip off for a few seconds and then lay on a cooling rack. Before the chocolate sets too much, sprinkle on some pretty sprinkles. You can now put these in the fridge to set for 30 minutes.

Next, mix up 3-4 tbsp of royal icing with a tsp or two of water. Keep adding water drop by drop until it is thick like melted chocolate. If it goes too runny, just add a little more royal icing until it's at the right consistency.

Pop this into a piping bag and snip a tiny bit off the end. Now drizzle a little royal icing over the other half of the biscuits. This will take around 20-30 minutes to set.

This yummy recipe is cross between a shortbread and a biscuit. Really delicious for decorating or just to dunk in a cup of tea. The biscuits will keep for 7-10 days and still taste gorgeous. Store in a biscuit tin or air tight container. You can also freeze these for 4-6 weeks and they still taste great.

PREPARATION

Preheat oven to
160 Fan

Prep
3x baking trays with baking paper

You'll Need
A large rolling pin

Optional
5mm spacers

INGREDIENTS

225g unsalted butter

190g caster sugar

2 tsp vanilla extract (optional. These taste great without it)

2 medium size eggs

420g Plain flour plus extra for rolling out

Mix together the butter and sugar until creamed and blended well.

Scrape down the mixing bowl and then add in the 2 eggs. Mix this up. Don't worry if it looks curdled. It's just due to the different temperatures of the ingredients. It'll be fine once the flour is added next.

So now add in the flour and mix until just combined. This will be a very thick dough and it's very tricky to mix properly when the flour is added.

Pour it all out onto a floured worktop and kneed for 1 minute. Use just enough flour so it doesn't feel sticky.

Ta-da....all done. You don't need to chill this recipe.

Next, decide on what number or letter you want. Create a template for this so each shape you make is the same (an internet image search of number/letter outline will do the job if you cant do this by hand)

Roll out your dough using 5mm spacers (or roll to 5mm if you can be precise without the spacers). Place your template on top and using a sharp knife cut around this. Remove the template and using your large cake scraper (as used on all the cakes) side under the shape, pick up and place on a lined flat baking tray. Repeat for 2 more shapes then bake in a preheated oven for 10-11 minutes. These are cooked when the cookie is just turning light brown on the egdes.

The cookie is very soft when taken out the oven so leave on the tray to cool completely then you can remove.

Once cooled, stack together with plain buttercream and complete your rainbow swirls, stars and ruffles on top (see all piping skills in the basics section)

DELICIOUS DONUTS

PREPARATION

Makes
12 Donuts

Preheat oven to
150 Fan

Prep
Spray 2 silicone donut pans with non stick spray.

INGREDIENTS

200g self raising flour

150g caster sugar

2 medium egg, lightly beaten

70ml whole milk

150g unsalted butter, melted

2 teaspoons vanilla extract

For the glaze topping

320g powdered sugar

4-5 tablespoons milk

Extras

Green, blue and purple food colouring

Mermaid sprinkles

These baked donuts are a fun alternative to fried donuts and make a great addition to a party cake. Easy to decorate with colours and sprinkles make it really simple to match the cake decor too. All the methods for making the donuts are the same but I've just created flavour variations for you. These are cooked on a slightly lower temperature than a cake as you want the donuts to rise but stay flatter.

In a mixer bowl, cream together the butter, sugar and vanilla for a minute or two until thoroughly mixed. Scrape the bowl down well. In a jug add together the milk and eggs and whisk. Add this into your butter mix and combine well. It may look curdled but don't worry, it'll be perfect after the next stage.

Next, add the flour. Continue to mix this up for 20-30 seconds until it looks smooth.

Put the donut batter into a piping bag and snip about an inch off the end. Pipe the batter into the donut mould until approx 3/4 full.

Cook in a preheated oven for around 18 minutes or until just going golden brown and coming away from the donut mould at the sides.

Leave to cool fully in the mould then transfer onto a wire rack.

Top tip - They can sometimes be a little bit of a pain to get out the mould. Make sure they are completely cooled. You can even pop them in the fridge for 10 minutes to cool further. Then peel back the silicone mould a little and holding the sides of the donut, gently twist a little and it'll pop out easy.

MAKE THE GLAZE

Add together all the glaze ingredients and whisk up. This should be very thick. When you stir it, it should take 20-25 seconds to become flat again in the bowl.

You can add in a few drops more of milk if you prefer but the thicker this is, the better it will cover the donuts. It'll cover any lumps and bumps of the bake and also stay on the top of the donut rather than all running over the edge.

To decorate with a mermaid theme, divide your glaze into 3 bowls and colour green, blue and purple. I used Colour Mill for this. Pour the glaze into piping bags with no nozzle.

Using one of your colours, snip a small amount off the end of the piping bag and pipe the glaze around the top edge of your donut and take this all the way to middle until covered.

Less is more with how much to add as this will spread out and cover more than the area you pipe.

Then take your second colour and pip a few lines across the top.

Do the same with your last colour. Then take a cocktail stick and swirl through the colours to combine.

Lastly, while the glaze is still wet, add on your sprinkles.

The glaze takes an hour or two to dry so leave them until completely dry.

Then you can eat up, set out on your party table or add into a treat box for family and friends. These are best eaten within 24/48 hours.

PREPARATION

Makes
12 Donuts

Preheat oven to
150 Fan

Prep
Spray 2 silicone donut
pans with non stick spray

INGREDIENTS

200g self raising flour

150g caster sugar

2 medium egg, lightly
  beaten

70ml whole milk

150g unsalted butter,
  melted

1 teaspoon cinnamon

1 teaspoon orange extract

1/2 orange zest

For the glaze topping

320g icing sugar

4-5 tablespoons milk

Optional: food colouring
  and sprinkles

In a mixer bowl, cream together the butter and sugar for a minute or two until thoroughly mixed. Scrape the bowl down well. In a jug add together the Orange extract, milk and eggs and whisk. Add this into your butter mix and combine well. It may look curdled but don't worry, it'll be perfect after the next stage.

Next, add the flour, orange zest and cinnamon. Continue to mix this up for 20-30 seconds until it looks smooth.

Put the batter into a piping bag and snip about an inch off the end. Pipe the batter into the donut mould until approx 3/4 full.

Cook in a preheated oven for around 18 minutes or until just going golden brown and coming away from the side of the donut mould.

Leave to cool fully in the mould then transfer onto a wire rack.

Top tip - They can sometimes be a little bit of a pain to get out the mould. Make sure they are completely cooled. You can even pop them int he fridge for 10 minutes to cool further. Then peel back the silicone a little and holding the sides of the donut, gently twist a little and it'll pop out easy.

Add together all the glaze ingredients and whisk up. This should be very thick. When you stir it, it should take 20-25 seconds to become flat again in the bowl.

You can add in a few drops more of milk if you prefer but the thicker this is, the better it will cover the donuts. It'll cover any lumps and bumps of the bake and also stay on the top of the donut rather than all running over the edge.

Add in some colour to part of your glaze. I used Colour mill pink. Make sure you leave a little of the glaze white for decorating.

Cover up the white glaze with some cling film until you are ready to use it.

Add the colour into a piping bag and snip a small amount off the end. Pipe the glaze around the top edge of your donut and take this all the way to middle until covered.

Less is more with how much to add as this will spread out and cover more than the area you pipe. Leave the donuts to set for an hour and then drizzle over the white glaze. Lastly, add on your sprinkles while the white glaze is still wet. These are best eaten within a day or two.

PREPARATION

Makes
12 Donuts

Preheat oven to
150 Fan

Prep
Spray 2 silicone donut pans with non stick spray

INGREDIENTS

175g self raising flour

25g cocoa powder

150g caster sugar

2 medium eggs, lightly beaten

70ml whole milk

150g unsalted butter, melted

1 teaspoons vanilla extract

1 tbsp golden syrup

Ganache topping

100g dark chocolate

80ml double cream

Extras

Chocolate sprinkles

In a mixer bowl, cream together the butter, sugar and vanilla for a minute or two until thoroughly mixed. Scrape the bowl down well. In a jug add together the milk, golden syrup and eggs then whisk. Add this into your butter mix and combine well. It may look curdled but don't worry, it'll be perfect after the next stage.

Next, add the flour and cocoa. Continue to mix this up for 20-30 seconds until it looks smooth.

Put the donut batter into a piping bag and snip about an inch off the end. Pipe the batter into the doubt mould until approx 3/4 full.

Cook in a preheated oven for around 10-12 minutes or the donuts feel touch dry on top.

Leave to cool fully in the mould then transfer onto a wire rack.

Top tip - They can sometimes be a little bit of a pain to get out the mould. Make sure they are completely cooled. You can even pop them in the fridge for 10 minutes to cool further. Then peel back the silicone a little and holding the sides of the donut, gently twist a little and it'll pop out easy.

Make the ganache topping. Pop the cream in a bowl and microwave for 30 seconds then stir. Pop back in the microwave again and for another 20-30 seconds until it hot but not boiling. Add in your chocolate to the bowl of cream and stir thoroughly. It should be almost melted. Pop back in the microwave for

10 seconds at a time and stir until melted.

Leave the ganache to cool for 30 minutes, stirring regularly. Then transfer into a piping bag. Pipe around the top edge of the donut then work towards the centre. The ganache will settle and become smooth. Before it dries, sprinkle on some sprinkles then leave to set.

These are best eaten within a day or two.

CHOCOLATE GOODIES

WHITE CHOCOLATE FRIDGE BAR

This fridge bar is insane. And I mean that in a very good way. So rich in flavour and one of my absolutely favourite recipes to make for a quick chocolate hit.

PREPARATION

Making Time
15-20 Minutes

Serves
16 Portions

Set Time
60+ Minutes

INGREDIENTS

125g butter

200g white chocolate chips

4tbsp Golden syrup

225g biscuits. (I love to use malted milk for this recipe)

200g white chocolate bars such as Caramc, milky bar, white chocolate twix, Hersheys, gold bars etc etc

Preparation - Start by lining a 8 x 8 square cake tin with baking paper. Cut up all your chocolate bars. Cut up the butter into cubes. Crush your biscuits.

In a saucepan on a low heat, gently melt the butter. Once melted, add in the golden syrup and chocolate, stirring constantly for 1 minute. Remove from the heat.

Add in all the crushed biscuits and chopped chocolate. Mix until the ingredients are evenly distributed and pour into baking tray.

Press flat with a tablespoon and top each section with something yummy. I used a white pretzel. You could use a slice of white chocolate or some extra chocolate chips.

Put this in the fridge and chill for 1-2 hours or until set.

When slicing this, it makes it really easy if you heat up a large knife in some hot water first. This will cut through the chocolate really easy.

Cut into 16 portions , stick the kettle on and enjoy!

This is by far the easiest thing to make. The variations are endless. I love creating these chocolate slabs. You can decorate for celebration snacks, bag up for easy and affordable party favours or just make some and have fun with the kids decorating them for a Friday night.

You'll need 150g chocolate for each type

And toppings - this could be sprinkles, chocolate, peanut butter, popcorn, fruit... The list is endless.

WHITE CHOCOLATE AND RASPBERRY SLAB

INGREDIENTS

150g white chocolate

Freeze dried fruit pieces

Melt the chocolate in the microwave for 30 second bursts until almost melted and stir well until completely melted. Prepare a baking tray with baking paper and then pour the chocolate in the middle of this. Using a spoon or palette knife slowly start to spread this chocolate out to 3-4 mm thick and create a rectangular shape.

Now it's time to add your toppings. I used some freeze dried fruit to team with the white chocolate. It makes a lovely fresh chocolate treat.

Set in the fridge for a few hours. Once set you can then break up into shards of chocolate ready to display or pop in a gift bag or box.

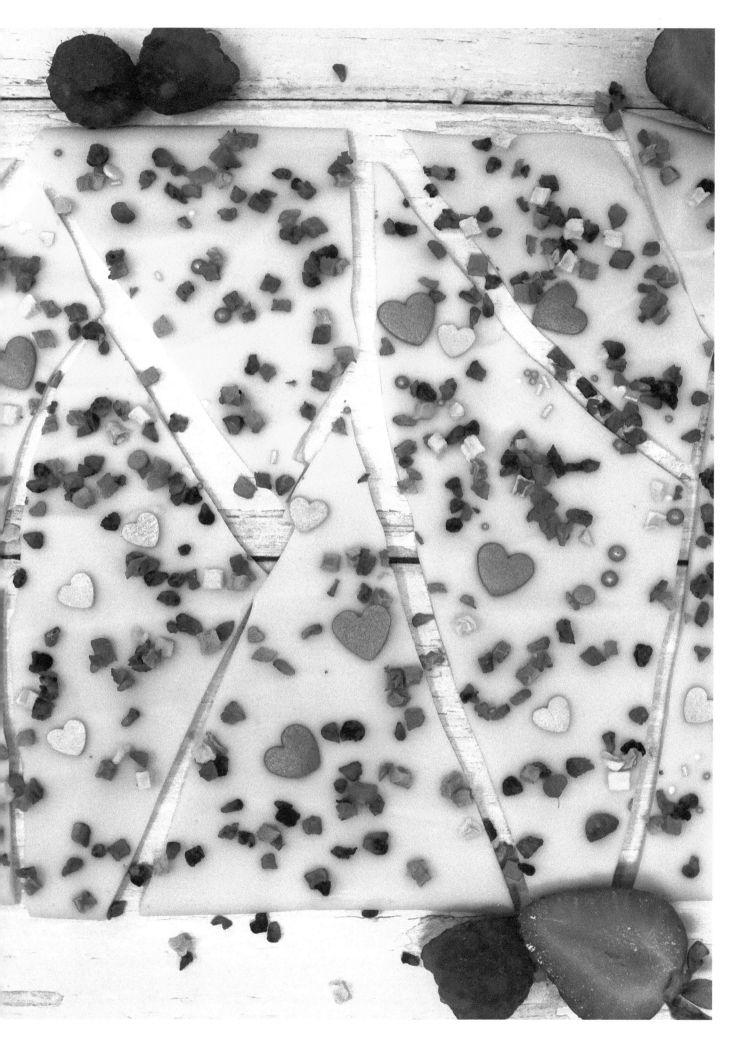

PEANUT BUTTER AND POPCORN SLAB

INGREDIENTS

30g dark chocolate

2 tbsp crunchy peanut butter

A handful of popcorn

150g milk chocolate

Melt the milk chocolate in the microwave for 30 second bursts until almost melted and stir well until completely melted. Prepare a baking tray with baking paper and then pour the chocolate in the middle of this. Using a spoon or palette knife slowly start to spread this chocolate out to 3-4 mm thick and create a rectangular shape.

Meanwhile, melt the peanut butter in the microwave for 10-15 seconds just to make it slightly runnier. Now drizzle this all over the dark chocolate and swirl through with a cocktail stick.

Sprinkle on some popcorn. Lastly, melt your dark chocolate, pop in a piping bag and drizzle this over the top to finish.

Now set in the fridge for 1-2 hours then break up into pieces ready to eat.

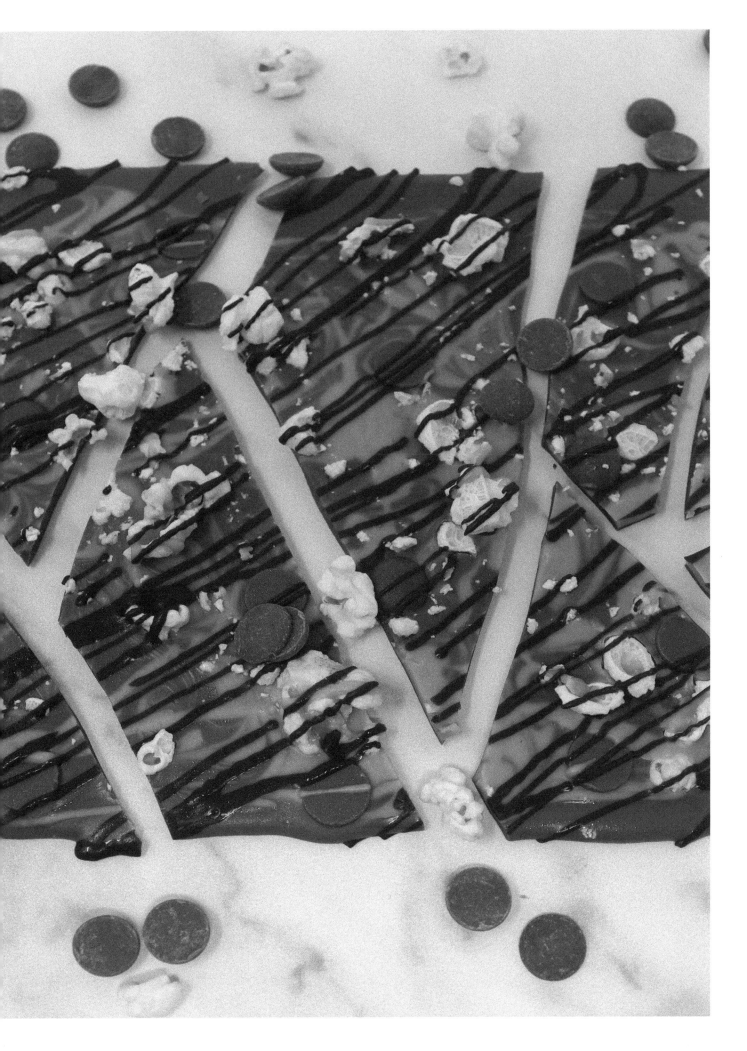

CHOCOLATE SPRINKLES SLAB

INGREDIENTS

150g milk chocolate

Edible sprinkles

Melt the chocolate in the microwave for 30 second bursts until almost melted and stir well until completely melted. Prepare a baking tray with baking paper and then pour the chocolate in the middle of this. Using a spoon or palette knife slowly start to spread this chocolate out to 3-4 mm thick and create a rectangular shape.

For these chocolate slabs, I added some gorgeous sprinkles from @super_streusel

Place in the fridge for a few hours to set. Once set you can then break up into shards of chocolate ready to display or pop in a gift bag or box.

BAKING QUANTITY CHART

It's always so helpful to have a conversion chart for baking various size tins. Here is mine that has never failed me yet. If you turn to my simple fresh vanilla cake page 58, this recipe chart is for this cake and works perfectly every time. This produces a lovely tall cake. Bake in a preheated oven at 160.

Baking Chart					
Tin size in inch		Each of butter, sugar and flour	Eggs	Vanilla extract in teaspoons	Baking time in mins
Round	Square				
4		250g	5	1.5	30
5	4	300g	6	2	35-40
6	5	350g	7	2	40
7	6	450g	9	2.5	45-50
8	7	500g	10	3	50-60
9	8	650g	13	3	60-70
10	9	800g	16	4	70-90
12	10	900g	18	5	80-90

My cupcake cases are coming away from my cupcakes.

Sadly this problem is all too common! The top causes are 1. Being under baked or not cooked. 2. Storing cupcakes in plastic containers (it makes them 'sweat').

My cupcakes are rising high and then sinking.

Make sure you don't open the oven door too soon. Try waiting a minute or two longer before opening the oven door next time. Also, check that you're adding the right amount of baking powder.

My cupcakes are rising unevenly.

Make sure that your baking powder is in date and evenly mixed in to your batter. Also check on your oven power. Use an oven thermometer to get an accurate temperature.

My cupcakes have a crusty top.

Be careful to make sure that you mix your sugar and eggs evenly through the whole batter. This often happens if we're in a bit of a rush and haven't quite combined everything. Also, your oven may be a little too hot and over cooking the top. Try turning down by 10 degrees

My cupcakes are dry.

Try baking them for 2 minutes less (and another 2 minutes less if the problem isn't fixed). Oh and remember fresh is always best! They will be dry if you eat them a week after making them, an unchangeable fact of life sadly!

My big cakes have a big crust.

Try baking them at a lower temperature for longer. They may take agggges to cook but it will almost certainly get rid of this problem.

My big cakes are dry.

Make sure you're not over baking them. Be careful to take them out of the oven when they are only just cooked.

My big cakes are sinking.

This is normally because the oven door was opened too soon. Or maybe because your oven isn't a true temperature. I'd recommend buying an oven thermometer and keeping watch on the reading. Watch out for these things! Also, make sure that the cake is fully cooked, if not it'll sink.

My cakes are dense and heavy.

This is caused when you over mix the batter. Just be sure to stop mixing as soon as the ingredients are combined.

A slice of cake has disappeared.

Ask your partner or kids. Check the dog. One of them will be the culprit!

@prop.options

These are my go to company for cake stands and styling props. They have such a brilliant range of stands and most stands I use are from here (unless I find a pretty one on my supermarket shop!)

@fox_and_moon

For all things planners and stationery, this company is brilliant. I also love supporting this lovely lady. She is a totally brilliant juggling motherhood and a busy business.

@bearcub.and.co

These girls sell an awesome range of cake toppers and cake charms

@super_streusel

A German based Sprinkle company who sell the most gorgeous sprinkle ranges. You can buy them in the UK from @cakecraftcompany

@colour.mill

For food colourings. I use these in my buttercream. The colours mix so well in this.

@cakestuffltd

My go to shop for all cake supplies. It's so good to have everything you need in one place. Not only that, the staff are so lovely and always helpful.

@sweet.stamp

They sell the most wonderful range of cake letter embossers and edible paints. I have got them and can highly recommend them.

@caketopperanimals

These gorgeous cake toppers are so unique. You can find them on my Jungle cake on page 78. You can personalise them with all kinds of colours, hats and accessories.

I teach so many cake skills and I love to teach anyone! Whether you have tons of experience or just starting out... I can help!

I teach online buttercream drip cakes, ruffles, big beautiful wedding cakes, indulgent chocolate cupcakes, sugar flowers and shaped cakes topped with flowers and hearts.

My cake business courses have gone global! I helped a lady set up her cake business in Canada last year, all over zoom.

I've been teaching cake classes since 2012. It's the best job in the world. I get to play cake all day teaching new cake friends new skills.

Now I'm not teaching in person we chat constantly on my Instagram, my Facebook page, student group and my cake chat group. We all keep in touch, sharing ideas, hints and tips. My social media is a place where I love to help them when they hit a cake problem and top them up with a little more cake confidence than they had before.

A huge cake filled thanks to everyone who constantly supports my business. The students who return again and again, even when they've already done that class before, who buy the online course when I've already taught them that technique, who sign up for my business courses and trust me to help their business bloom and everyone who likes, comments and shares my social media posts. It never goes unnoticed. Those little acts of support go a long way and I'll be forever grateful.

CPSIA information can be obtained
at www.ICGtesting.com
Printed in the USA
BVHW020225270321
603523BV00016B/1178